Table Of Contents

I0427446

Chapter 1 - Understanding the Need
for Career Transitions   6

  The Evolving Landscape of
Careers   6

  The Challenges Faced by
Athletes, First Responders, Mid
Career Professionals, Lawyers, and
Doctors   8

  The Importance of Career
Transitions for Personal Growth and
Fulfillment   10

Chapter 2 - Assessing Your Skills and
Interests   13

  Identifying Transferable Skills
from Your Current Career   13

  Exploring Your Interests and
Passions   15

  Conducting Self-Assessments and
Skill Inventories   17

Chapter 3 - Researching Alternative
Career Paths   20

  Exploring Different Industries and
Sectors   20

Investigating Job Market Trends
and Opportunities 22

Networking and Gathering
Informational Interviews 24

Chapter 4 - Setting Clear Goals and
Objectives 27

Defining Your Long-Term Career
Vision 27

Setting Short-Term and
Intermediate Goals 29

Creating an Action Plan 31

Chapter 5 - Developing New Skills
and Knowledge 34

Identifying Skill Gaps and Training
Needs 34

Pursuing Further Education and
Certifications 36

Leveraging Online Learning
Platforms and Resources 38

Chapter 6 - Building a Professional
Network 41

Expanding Your Network Within
Your Current Field 41

Reaching out to Industry
Professionals in Your Desired Career
Path 43

Utilizing Social Media and
Networking Events   45

Chapter 7 - Crafting a Compelling
Resume and Cover Letter   48

Showcasing Transferable Skills
and Accomplishments   48

Tailoring Your Resume for
Different Job Applications   50

Writing an Engaging Cover Letter   52

Chapter 8 - Mastering the Job Search
Process   55

Utilizing Job Search Websites and
Platforms   55

Leveraging Recruitment Agencies
and Headhunters   57

Navigating the Hidden Job Market   59

Chapter 9 - Acing Interviews and
Negotiating Job Offers   61

Preparing for Different Types of
Interviews   61

Answering Common Interview
Questions   63

Negotiating Salary, Benefits, and
Work-Life Balance   66

Chapter 10 - Thriving in Your New
Career   68

Onboarding and Adjusting to a
New Work Environment   68

Building Rapport with Colleagues
and Superiors   70

Continuously Learning and
Growing in Your New Role   72

Chapter 11 - Overcoming Challenges
and Staying Resilient   75

Dealing with Imposter Syndrome
and Self-Doubt   75

Managing Setbacks and
Rejections   77

Maintaining Work-Life Balance in
a New Career   79

Chapter 12 - Continuing Professional
Development and Growth   82

Seeking Mentorship and Coaching
Opportunities   82

Pursuing Additional Training and
Certifications   84

Staying Updated with Industry
Trends and Best Practices   87

Chapter 13 - Inspiring Success
Stories and Lessons Learned   90

Athletes Who Successfully
Transitioned to New Careers   90

First Responders Who Found
Fulfillment in Alternative Paths   92

Mid-career professionals,
Lawyers, and Doctors Who Made
Successful Transitions   94

Chapter 14 - Creating a Sustainable
and Fulfilling Career Path   97

Aligning Your Career with Your
Personal Values and Passions   97

Embracing Lifelong Learning and
Adaptability   99

Finding Fulfillment and
Satisfaction in Your Chosen Path   101

Conclusion - Your Playbook for
Athlete Career Transitions   104

Chapter 1 – Understanding the Need for Career Transitions

The Evolving Landscape of Careers

In today's dynamic and ever-changing world, career paths are no longer linear. Gone are the days when individuals would choose one profession and stick with it for their entire working lives. The landscape of careers is evolving rapidly, and it is crucial for athletes, first responders, mid-career professionals, lawyers, and doctors to be aware of the shifts and opportunities that lie ahead.

How To Change Career Paths

Career transitions can be both exciting and daunting. Whether you are an athlete reaching the end of your playing days, a first responder looking for a change of pace, a mid-career professional seeking new challenges, or a lawyer or doctor considering alternative paths, this chapter will guide you through the process of changing career paths with ease and confidence.

One of the first steps in changing career paths is self-reflection. Take the time to assess your skills, interests, and values. What are your strengths? What brings you joy and fulfillment? Understanding yourself and your motivations will help you identify potential career paths that align with your passions.

Next, research various industries and professions that pique your interest. The evolving landscape of careers offers a plethora of options to explore. Look for emerging fields and trends that align with your skills and interests. Consider the skills you have acquired in your current profession and how they can be transferable to new roles. This will help you identify where your expertise can be applied in different contexts.

Once you have identified potential career paths, it is crucial to invest in your professional development. Upskilling and reskilling are essential in today's rapidly changing job market. Use online courses, workshops, and networking opportunities to stay updated with the latest industry trends and expand your knowledge base.

Networking is another critical aspect of changing career paths. Connect with professionals in your desired field, attend industry events, and join relevant communities. Build relationships, seek mentorship, and learn from those who have successfully transitioned into similar roles.

Embrace a growth mindset and be open to new possibilities. Changing career paths can be challenging, but it also presents an opportunity for personal and professional growth. Embrace the unknown, stay adaptable, and be willing to take calculated risks.

The evolving landscape of careers presents a multitude of opportunities for athletes, first responders, mid-career professionals, lawyers, and doctors to change career paths. By engaging in self-reflection, conducting thorough research, investing in professional development, networking, and embracing a growth mindset, individuals can navigate these transitions successfully. Embrace the endless possibilities that lie ahead and embark on a fulfilling and rewarding new career journey.

The Challenges Faced by Athletes, First Responders, Mid Career Professionals, Lawyers, and Doctors

Career transitions can be daunting and challenging for anyone, regardless of their profession. However, certain professions, such as athletes, first responders, mid-career professionals, lawyers, and doctors, face unique obstacles when attempting to change their career paths. In this subchapter, we will explore the specific challenges that individuals in these professions encounter and provide guidance on navigating these transitions successfully.

For athletes, transitioning from a career in sports can be emotionally and mentally taxing. The sudden loss of identity, the pressure to find a new purpose, and the uncertainty of what lies ahead can be overwhelming. Moreover, athletes often struggle with transferring their skills and finding industries that align with their values and interests. This chapter will delve into strategies for self-reflection, skill assessment, and exploring new career opportunities that are suitable for athletes.

First responders, including police officers, firefighters, and paramedics, face the challenge of leaving a profession that is deeply ingrained in their identities. The transition from a high-stress, high-stakes job to a new career path can be difficult, as first responders often have specialized skills that may not directly translate to other industries. This section will provide insights on leveraging transferable skills, seeking additional education or certifications, and exploring alternative careers within the public service sector.

Mid-career professionals often find themselves at a crossroads, feeling stuck or unfulfilled in their current roles. The challenge lies in identifying new career paths that align with their interests and skills without feeling like they are starting from scratch. This subchapter will provide guidance on self-assessment, exploring new industries, networking, and leveraging past experiences to facilitate a smooth career transition.

Lawyers and doctors, despite their highly specialized professions, are not immune to the desire for a change in career. However, they face unique challenges, including the extensive educational and professional commitments they have made in their respective fields. This section will offer practical advice on identifying transferrable skills, exploring non-traditional legal or medical careers, and seeking additional education or certifications to facilitate a successful career transition.

No matter the profession, changing career paths can be both exhilarating and challenging. This subchapter aims to provide guidance and support to athletes, first responders, mid-career professionals, lawyers, and doctors who are contemplating a career change. By addressing the specific challenges faced by these individuals and offering practical tips and strategies, this book seeks to empower its readers to successfully navigate their career transitions and find fulfillment in their new paths.

The Importance of Career Transitions for Personal Growth and Fulfillment

In today's fast-paced and ever-changing world, career transitions have become more common than ever before. Whether you are an athlete, a first responder, a mid-career professional, a lawyer, or a doctor, there may come a time when you feel the need to change your career path.

This subchapter of "The Playbook for Athlete Career Transitions - A Step-by-Step Guide" explores why career transitions are crucial for personal growth and fulfillment and provides valuable insights for individuals in various niches on navigating these transitions successfully.

One of the primary reasons career transitions are essential is personal growth. When individuals step out of their comfort zones and embrace new challenges, they open themselves up to new experiences, knowledge, and skills. Transitioning careers allows individuals to break free from the monotony of their current roles and explore different avenues of personal and professional development. By exposing themselves to new environments, individuals can broaden their perspectives, enhance their problem-solving abilities, and build resilience, which are all vital for personal growth.

Furthermore, career transitions often lead to greater fulfillment. Many individuals find themselves feeling unfulfilled or stuck in their current careers, which can negatively impact their mental and emotional well-being. By making a change, individuals can align their jobs with their passions, values, and aspirations. This alignment fosters a sense of purpose and fulfillment, ultimately leading to greater satisfaction in both personal and professional lives.

For athletes, first responders, mid-career professionals, lawyers, and doctors, transitioning careers may seem daunting. However, this subchapter provides a step-by-step guide to navigate career transitions successfully. It offers practical advice on how to identify transferable skills, explore alternative career paths, acquire additional qualifications if necessary, network effectively, create a compelling resume, and ace interviews in new industries.

This subchapter emphasizes the importance of seeking support during career transitions. It encourages individuals to tap into their existing networks, join professional associations, and seek mentorship to gain guidance and leverage the experiences of others who have successfully transitioned careers.

areer transitions are essential for personal growth and fulfillment. Whether you are an athlete, a first responder, a mid-career professional, a lawyer, or a doctor, embracing career transitions can open doors to new experiences, personal development, and increased satisfaction. By following the step-by-step guide provided in this subchapter, individuals can confidently navigate career transitions and embark on a fulfilling and rewarding new path.

Chapter 2 – Assessing Your Skills and Interests

Identifying Transferable Skills from Your Current Career

Subchapter - Identifying Transferable Skills from Your Current Career

In today's fast-paced and ever-changing world, career transitions have become increasingly common and necessary. Whether you are an athlete looking to transition into a new career, a first responder contemplating a different path, a mid-career professional seeking a change, or a lawyer or doctor considering a career shift, this subchapter is designed to help you identify and leverage your transferable skills.

Transitioning from one career to another can be intimidating, but it doesn't have to be overwhelming. By recognizing the skills you have developed in your current job, you can confidently navigate the process of changing career paths. Here's how -

1. Self-reflection - Start by reflecting on your current career and the skills you have acquired. Consider the tasks, responsibilities, and challenges you have faced. What skills have you developed as a result? These could include leadership, teamwork, problem-solving, adaptability, communication, and many others.

2. Analyze job descriptions - Look for job descriptions in your desired field and carefully read through the required skills and qualifications. Compare these with the skills you have identified from your current career. You may be surprised to find that you possess many of the skills sought after in your new job.

3. Seek feedback - Reach out to mentors, colleagues, or professionals in your desired field to gain their perspective on your transferable skills. Their insights can help you validate your own assessment and provide valuable guidance on how to position yourself for a successful transition.

4. Skills mapping - Create a skills map that visually represents the skills you have developed in your current career and how they align with the skills required in your desired field. This map will serve as a valuable tool during interviews and networking opportunities, showcasing the value you bring to the table.

5. Continuous learning - Identify any gaps in your skill set and actively seek opportunities to bridge them. This may involve taking courses, attending workshops, or pursuing certifications. Emphasize your commitment to learning and growth when discussing your transferable skills with potential employers.

Remember, changing career paths is not about starting from scratch; it's about leveraging the skills and experiences you already possess. By identifying and highlighting your transferable skills, you can confidently navigate the process of transitioning into a new career. Embrace the challenge, embrace the opportunity, and embrace the potential for personal and professional growth.

Whether you are an athlete, first responder, mid-career professional, lawyer, or doctor, this subchapter will provide you with the tools and strategies needed to successfully change career paths.

Exploring Your Interests and Passions

In the journey of career transitions, it is crucial to take the time to explore your interests and passions. For athletes, first responders, mid-career professionals, lawyers, and doctors, who are contemplating a change in their career paths, this subchapter aims to guide you in discovering what truly ignites your curiosity and enthusiasm.

One of the first steps in exploring your interests and passions is to reflect on your current career. Ask yourself what aspects of your current profession bring you joy and fulfillment. Are there any specific tasks or responsibilities that you excel at and enjoy doing? This self-reflection will help you identify skills and strengths that can be transferred to a new career path.

Next, delve into activities outside of your professional life that bring you happiness. Explore hobbies, volunteer opportunities, or side projects that you find intriguing. Engaging in activities beyond your day job allows you to discover new interests and develop skills that may be valuable in a different career field. Keep an open mind and be willing to step out of your comfort zone to explore new territories.

Networking is another powerful tool for exploring your interests and passions. Reach out to professionals in fields that interest you and request informational interviews. These conversations can provide insights into different career paths and help you determine if a particular industry aligns with your interests. Additionally, attending industry conferences, workshops, and networking events can expose you to a wide range of possibilities and connect you with like-minded individuals.

Consider seeking guidance from career coaches or mentors specializing in career transitions. These experts can provide valuable advice, help you identify your strengths, and guide you toward potential opportunities that align with your interests. They can also assist in developing a strategic plan for your career change, ensuring a smooth transition.

Be patient and embrace the journey. Exploring your interests and passions is not a linear process and may take time.

Exploring your interests and passions is a vital step in changing career paths. By reflecting on your current career, engaging in new activities, networking, seeking guidance, and being patient, you can uncover new possibilities and find a fulfilling career that aligns with your passions and interests. Remember, this is your playbook for a successful career transition, and exploring your interests and desires is a significant chapter within it.

Conducting Self-Assessments and Skill Inventories

In today's rapidly changing world, career transitions have become a common phenomenon.

Athletes, first responders, mid-career professionals, lawyers, and doctors often find themselves at a crossroads, contemplating a shift in their career paths. However, embarking on a new journey requires careful self-reflection and an understanding of one's skills and abilities. This subchapter, "Conducting Self-Assessments and Skill Inventories," aims to guide individuals through the process of evaluating themselves and determining their transferable skills as they navigate the challenging terrain of career change.

Self-assessments serve as the foundation for any successful transition. They provide a comprehensive analysis of an individual's strengths, weaknesses, interests, and values. Athletes, first responders, mid-career professionals, lawyers, and doctors bring unique skill sets to the table, acquired through years of dedication and training. However, these skills may not always align with their desired career paths. Therefore, it is crucial to assess personal interests and identify transferrable skills that can be leveraged in new industries.

Skill inventories play a pivotal role in this process. By meticulously listing skills developed throughout one's current career and personal life, individuals gain a clear understanding of their capabilities. Whether it's leadership, problem-solving, teamwork, or communication, these skills often transcend industries and can be utilized in various contexts. Recognizing these transferable skills lays the foundation for a successful career transition.

This subchapter delves into the importance of conducting a gap analysis. By comparing desired career paths with current skill sets, individuals gain insight into areas where they may need to acquire additional knowledge or expertise. This analysis acts as a roadmap for professional development, guiding individuals towards courses, certifications, or networking opportunities that can bridge the gaps and enhance their employability.

Additionally, the subchapter emphasizes the significance of seeking guidance and support during this period of transformation. It provides strategies for building a solid network, engaging with mentors, and seeking professional advice. Sharing experiences with like-minded individuals who have undergone similar career transitions can provide valuable insights and motivation.

"Conducting Self-Assessments and Skill Inventories" is an essential subchapter in "The Playbook for Athlete Career Transitions - A Step-by-Step Guide." It provides athletes, first responders, mid-career professionals, lawyers, and doctors with the tools and knowledge needed to navigate the challenging process of changing career paths. By conducting thorough self-assessments, identifying transferable skills, and bridging gaps, individuals can successfully transition into new industries and embark on fulfilling and rewarding careers.

Chapter 3 – Researching Alternative Career Paths

Exploring Different Industries and Sectors

In today's rapidly changing world, career transitions have become increasingly common. Athletes, first responders, mid-career professionals, lawyers, and doctors often find themselves contemplating a change in their career paths. However, making such a transition can be daunting, especially when considering the vast array of industries and sectors available.

This subchapter aims to guide individuals through the process of exploring different industries and sectors as they embark on a career change. By providing a step-by-step approach, this chapter will help athletes, first responders, mid-career professionals, lawyers, and doctors gain clarity and confidence in their decision-making.

The first step in exploring different industries and sectors is self-reflection. It is essential to assess one's skills, interests, values, and long-term goals. This reflective exercise will help individuals identify industries and sectors that align with their passions and strengths.

Next, it is crucial to conduct thorough research on the potential industries of interest. This involves gathering information about the job market, growth prospects, required skills, and educational requirements. Engaging in informational interviews or shadowing professionals in the desired industries can provide valuable insights and help individuals make informed decisions.

Once a few industries and sectors have been identified, it is beneficial to delve deeper into understanding the intricacies of each. This includes exploring the various job roles, responsibilities, and potential career paths within these industries. Additionally, individuals should consider the possible challenges and rewards associated with each sector, as well as the lifestyle implications.

Networking plays a vital role in career transitions. Building connections with professionals already working in the desired industries can open doors to new opportunities. Attending industry events, joining relevant associations, and leveraging online platforms can facilitate meaningful connections and provide access to insider knowledge.

Individuals are encouraged to seek guidance from career coaches or mentors specializing in career transitions. These professionals can provide valuable advice, assist in developing a strategic plan, and offer support throughout the transition process.

By exploring different industries and sectors, athletes, first responders, mid-career professionals, lawyers, and doctors can expand their horizons and discover new career paths that align with their skills, interests, and aspirations. With careful consideration, thorough research, and the support of the right resources, a successful career transition is within reach for anyone willing to embark on this journey.

Investigating Job Market Trends and Opportunities

In today's rapidly evolving job market, staying informed about the latest trends and opportunities is crucial for individuals considering a career transition. Whether you are an athlete, a first responder, a mid-career professional, a lawyer, or a doctor, understanding how to change career paths effectively can open doors to new and exciting possibilities. This subchapter aims to provide you with valuable insights on investigating job market trends and opportunities, equipping you with the necessary tools to make informed decisions about your professional future.

To begin this journey, it is essential to recognize the importance of conducting thorough research. Start by exploring current job market trends in your desired industry or field. Pay attention to emerging sectors, technological advancements, and the skills that are in high demand. This research will enable you to identify potential job opportunities, understand the skill sets required, and align your own skills and experiences accordingly.

Networking plays a pivotal role in discovering hidden job market opportunities. Connect with professionals from various industries through networking events, conferences, or online platforms. Engage in conversations, seek advice, and learn from their experiences. By building and nurturing relationships, you may gain access to job openings that are not publicly advertised. Networking can also provide valuable insights into the skills and qualifications that employers are seeking, enabling you to tailor your career transition accordingly.

Consider seeking guidance from career coaches or mentors specializing in career transitions. These experts can provide you with invaluable advice, help you identify transferable skills, and guide you through the process of exploring new career paths. They can also assist in refining your resume, preparing for interviews, and developing a strategic job search plan.

Staying updated on industry-specific news and publications is essential. Subscribe to relevant newsletters, join professional organizations, and follow influential figures in your desired field on social media platforms. This will keep you informed about the latest industry trends, job market demands, and emerging opportunities.

Investigating job market trends and opportunities is a vital step towards successfully changing career paths. By conducting comprehensive research, networking effectively, seeking guidance from experts, and staying updated on industry news, you can position yourself to capitalize on the ever-evolving job market. Embrace this subchapter as your playbook for navigating the exciting world of career transitions and unlocking new doors to a fulfilling and successful professional future.

Networking and Gathering Informational Interviews

In today's competitive job market, networking and gathering informational interviews have become essential tools for individuals looking to change their career paths. Whether you are an athlete, first responder, mid-career professional, lawyer, or doctor, understanding how to network and conduct informational interviews effectively can significantly increase your chances of successfully transitioning into a new career.

Networking is the art of building relationships and connections with professionals in your desired industry. It involves reaching out to individuals through various platforms such as social media, professional networking events, or even personal connections.

By networking, you can tap into the hidden job market, which consists of job opportunities that are not publicly advertised. This can give you a distinct advantage over other candidates who rely solely on traditional job applications. Athletes, first responders, mid-career professionals, lawyers, and doctors can leverage their existing network of colleagues, friends, and mentors to expand their professional connections.

Informational interviews are an invaluable tool for gathering industry-specific knowledge and insights. These interviews allow you to connect with professionals who are already working in your desired field and gain a deeper understanding of their experiences, challenges, and successes. By conducting informational interviews, you can uncover potential career opportunities, build relationships with industry experts, and gather advice on how to navigate your career change successfully.

To effectively network and conduct informational interviews, it is essential to approach each interaction with a clear purpose and genuine curiosity. Prepare a list of questions and research the individuals you will speak with to demonstrate your interest and professionalism. Remember to listen actively and take notes during the conversations to gather valuable information and make a positive impression.

Utilizing online platforms such as LinkedIn can significantly enhance your networking efforts. Create a compelling profile that highlights your skills, experiences, and career goals. Join relevant groups and engage in discussions to increase your visibility within your desired industry. By actively participating in online communities, you can connect with professionals who share similar interests and expand your network even further.

Networking and gathering informational interviews require dedication and persistence. It may take time to establish meaningful connections and find individuals willing to share their insights. However, by consistently reaching out, attending networking events, and leveraging your existing network, you can create valuable connections that will significantly contribute to your successful career transition.

Networking and gathering informational interviews are crucial steps in changing career paths for athletes, first responders, mid-career professionals, lawyers, and doctors. By actively networking and conducting informational interviews, you can tap into hidden job opportunities, gain industry-specific knowledge, and build meaningful connections with professionals in your desired field. Embrace these strategies, and open yourself up to a world of career possibilities.

Chapter 4 – Setting Clear Goals and Objectives

Defining Your Long-Term Career Vision

In today's rapidly changing world, it is becoming increasingly common for individuals to change career paths multiple times throughout their lives. Whether you are an athlete looking to transition into a new field, a first responder seeking a change, a mid-career professional considering a new direction, or even a lawyer or doctor contemplating a shift, defining your long-term career vision is a crucial step in successfully navigating a career transition.

When embarking on a new career path, having a clear vision of where you want to go and what you want to achieve is essential. It serves as a guiding light, helping you make informed decisions and focus on your goals. Without a well-defined vision, you risk wandering aimlessly and feeling unfulfilled in your professional life.

To begin defining your long-term career vision, start by reflecting on your passions, interests, and values. Consider what brings you joy and fulfillment outside of your current career. Are there any specific industries or fields that have always intrigued you? Are there any causes or issues that you are deeply passionate about? Identifying these elements will allow you to align your career choices with your personal values and interests.

Next, take the time to research different career paths that align with your passions and interests. Consider reaching out to professionals in those fields to gain insight into the day-to-day realities, required skills, and potential opportunities. This research will help you gain a better understanding of the possibilities available to you and allow you to make informed decisions about your future.

Once you have gathered this information, create a vision statement that encapsulates your long-term career goals. Your vision statement should be concise, inspiring, and specific. It should paint a clear picture of what you want to achieve and why it matters to you. This vision statement will serve as a constant reminder of your aspirations and will help you stay motivated during challenging times.

As you progress in your career transition, remember that your long-term career vision is not set in stone. It may evolve and change as you gain new experiences and insights. Embrace the process of exploration and self-discovery, and be open to adjusting your vision when necessary.

By defining your long-term career vision, you are taking a proactive step toward creating a fulfilling and rewarding professional life. It will serve as your guidepost, helping you navigate the challenges and uncertainties that come with changing career paths. So, take the time to reflect, and define your vision – your future self will thank you for it.

Setting Short-Term and Intermediate Goals

In the journey of transitioning from one career path to another, setting short-term and intermediate goals is crucial for success. Whether you are an athlete looking to transition into a new career, a first responder seeking a change, or a mid-career professional, lawyer, or doctor exploring new opportunities, this chapter will guide you through the process of setting practical goals.

Short-term goals provide the stepping stones toward your long-term aspirations. They are the smaller, manageable objectives that act as building blocks for your overall career transition. These goals are typically achievable within a few weeks or months and serve as a way to measure progress and keep you motivated.

To begin, take some time to reflect on your long-term career goals. What do you envision yourself doing in the future? Where do you see yourself in five or ten years? Once you have a clear vision, break it down into smaller milestones to work towards.

When setting short-term goals, it's essential to make them specific, measurable, attainable, relevant, and time-bound (SMART). For example, if you are an athlete transitioning into a career in finance, a short-term goal could be to complete an online course in financial analysis within the next three months.

This goal is specific, measurable (completing the course), attainable (through online learning), relevant (to your desired career path), and time-bound (within three months).

Intermediate goals, on the other hand, are the stepping stones between your short-term goals and long-term aspirations. They are typically achieved within a year or two and help you stay focused and motivated along the way. These goals should align with your overall career transition plan and provide a sense of direction.

An example of an intermediate goal for a mid-career professional looking to become an entrepreneur could be to develop a comprehensive business plan within the next twelve months. This goal sets the groundwork for future endeavors and helps you move closer to your long-term vision.

Remember, setting short-term and intermediate goals is not a one-time task. As you progress in your career transition, reassess and adjust your goals accordingly. Celebrate each milestone achieved, and use setbacks as opportunities for growth and learning. With a clear vision and well-defined goals, you will be well-equipped to navigate your way through your career transition and successfully embark on a new path.

Creating an Action Plan

In today's dynamic and unpredictable job market, the need to change career paths can arise for various reasons. Whether you are an athlete looking to transition into a new profession, a first responder seeking a change, a mid-career professional considering a different industry, or even a lawyer or doctor contemplating a career shift, having a well-defined action plan is essential to ensure a smooth and successful transition. In this subchapter, we will outline the critical steps involved in creating an action plan to help you navigate the process of changing career paths.

1. Self-Reflection - Begin by conducting a thorough self-assessment to identify your skills, interests, values, and strengths. Consider what motivates and excites you, as well as what you envision for your future career. This introspection will provide valuable insights in determining the direction you want to pursue.

2. Research - Once you have a clear idea of your goals, start researching potential career paths that align with your interests and skill set. Explore industries, job roles, and organizations that appeal to you, and gather information about the qualifications, required training, and expected growth opportunities in those fields.

3. Networking - Networking is crucial in any career transition. Reach out to professionals in your desired field, attend industry events, and join relevant online communities. Building connections will not only provide you with valuable advice and insights but also potentially open doors to opportunities you may not have otherwise discovered.

4. Skill Development - Identify any gaps in your skill set and consider pursuing additional education, certifications, or training to make yourself more competitive in your desired field. Leverage your existing strengths and transferable skills to showcase your potential as a valuable asset to employers.

5. Set Goals - Establish short-term and long-term goals that are specific, measurable, achievable, relevant, and time-bound (SMART goals). Break down these goals into actionable steps and create a timeline to keep yourself accountable.

6. Update Your Resume and Online Presence - Tailor your resume to highlight relevant experiences and transferable skills for your new career path. Ensure that your online presence, including your LinkedIn profile and professional website, accurately reflects your new direction.

7. Seek Mentorship and Guidance - Engage with mentors or career coaches who can provide guidance, support, and advice throughout your career transition. Their experience and insights can prove invaluable during this process.

8. Take Action - Execute your action plan diligently, leveraging the knowledge, skills, and connections you have acquired. Be proactive in seeking out opportunities and be open to taking calculated risks.

Remember, changing career paths is a journey that requires patience, persistence, and adaptability. By following these steps and creating a well-defined action plan, you will be better equipped to navigate the challenges and maximize your chances of a successful career transition.

Chapter 5 – Developing New Skills and Knowledge

Identifying Skill Gaps and Training Needs

In the ever-evolving professional landscape, career transitions have become increasingly common. Whether you are an athlete seeking new avenues after retirement, a first responder looking to explore different career paths, a mid-career professional contemplating a change, or even a lawyer or doctor considering a new direction, identifying skill gaps and training needs is crucial to navigating a career transition successfully. This subchapter aims to provide you with a step-by-step guide on how to identify these gaps and effectively address your training needs.

The first step in identifying skill gaps is to conduct a thorough self-assessment. Take the time to reflect on your strengths, weaknesses, and interests. Consider your previous experiences, both within your current profession and outside of it. This self-reflection will allow you to pinpoint the skills you possess and those you lack.

Next, research the desired career path you wish to pursue. Understand the skills and qualifications required for success in that field. Look for job descriptions, talk to professionals already working in that field, and join relevant industry networks or associations. This research will help you identify the skill gaps between your current skill set and what is required in your desired career.

Once you have identified the skill gaps, it is time to address your training needs. This can be done through various means, depending on your specific circumstances. Consider enrolling in formal education programs, such as college courses, vocational training, or certification programs. These can provide you with the necessary knowledge and credentials to succeed in your new career path.

Seek out on-the-job training opportunities, internships, or apprenticeships. These hands-on experiences will allow you to gain practical skills and knowledge while working alongside professionals in your desired field.

Explore online resources, webinars, workshops, and seminars related to your target industry. These can provide valuable insights and training in a convenient and flexible manner.

Don't underestimate the power of networking. Connect with professionals in your desired field, attend industry events, and engage in mentorship programs. Building relationships and seeking guidance from experienced individuals can help bridge the gap between your current skill set and the skills required in your new career.

Identifying skill gaps and training needs is a crucial step in successfully changing career paths. By conducting a self-assessment, researching your desired field, and addressing your training needs through various means, such as formal education, on-the-job training, online resources, and networking, you can equip yourself with the skills necessary for a smooth transition. Remember, with the right mindset and dedication, you can embrace new opportunities and thrive in your chosen career path.

Pursuing Further Education and Certifications

In today's rapidly evolving job market, the importance of continuous learning and professional development cannot be emphasized enough. Whether you are an athlete looking to transition into a new career, a first responder exploring alternative paths, a mid-career professional seeking growth opportunities, or even a lawyer or doctor considering a change, further education and certifications can be the key to unlocking new possibilities and advancing your career.

One of the most effective ways to change career paths is by acquiring new skills and knowledge through further education. This may involve pursuing a degree program, attending workshops and seminars, or enrolling in online courses. The beauty of education is that it opens doors to new industries and expands your professional network, enabling you to connect with like-minded individuals and potential employers.

Another avenue to consider is obtaining professional certifications. Certifications demonstrate your expertise in a specific field and can enhance your credibility, making you a valuable asset to prospective employers. For example, if you are an athlete interested in transitioning into the fitness industry, obtaining certifications as a personal trainer or fitness instructor can provide you with the necessary qualifications to pursue a career in that field.

Continuing education and certifications offer the opportunity to stay up-to-date with the latest industry trends and advancements. This is particularly crucial in fields such as technology, healthcare, and law, where knowledge and skills quickly become outdated. By investing in your professional development, you not only stay relevant but also position yourself as a sought-after professional in your chosen niche.

It's important to note that pursuing further education and certifications requires dedication, time, and financial commitment. However, the long-term benefits far outweigh the temporary sacrifices. When considering a career change, take the time to research the educational requirements and certifications relevant to your desired field. Explore various learning options, including traditional institutions, online platforms, and professional organizations offering specialized courses.

Remember, the journey to a successful career transition is not a sprint but a marathon. Commit yourself to lifelong learning, embrace new challenges, and seize every opportunity to expand your knowledge and skill set. By pursuing further education and certifications, you are setting yourself up for success in your new career path. So, lace up your shoes, grab your playbook, and embark on this exciting journey toward a fulfilling and rewarding professional life.

Leveraging Online Learning Platforms and Resources

In today's rapidly evolving world, the ability to adapt and change career paths has become a valuable skill. Whether you are an athlete looking to transition into a new profession, a first responder seeking a change, a mid-career professional wanting to explore new opportunities, or even a lawyer or doctor seeking a different career path, online learning platforms, and resources can be your ultimate game-changer.

Online learning has revolutionized the way we acquire knowledge and skills. With the click of a button, you can access a vast array of courses, programs, and resources tailored to your specific interests and career goals. These platforms offer flexibility, convenience, and affordability, making them an ideal choice for individuals looking to make a successful career transition.

One of the key advantages of online learning platforms is the ability to learn at your own pace. As an athlete, first responder, mid-career professional, lawyer, or doctor, you have unique demands on your time. Online courses allow you to balance your existing commitments while gaining new skills and knowledge. You can study during your free time, whether it's early mornings, late nights, or weekends, without having to compromise your current responsibilities.

Online learning platforms offer a wide range of courses and programs to cater to various career paths. Whether you want to explore an entirely new field or enhance your existing skills, there is a course or program available for you. From business management and marketing to coding and design, these platforms cover almost every niche you can imagine.

Another benefit of leveraging online learning resources is the opportunity to learn from industry experts and thought leaders. Many platforms collaborate with top universities and professionals to provide high-quality content. This ensures that you receive the most up-to-date information and insights from experts in the field. You can also interact with fellow learners, join discussion forums, and network with like-minded individuals, creating valuable connections that can support your career transition.

Online learning platforms and resources have opened up endless possibilities for athletes, first responders, mid-career professionals, lawyers, and doctors seeking to change career paths. They provide the flexibility, convenience, and affordability needed to acquire new skills and knowledge at your own pace. By leveraging these platforms, you can gain a competitive edge in your desired field, opening doors to exciting new opportunities and ensuring a successful career transition.

Chapter 6 - Building a Professional Network

Expanding Your Network Within Your Current Field

In today's competitive job market, networking has become an essential tool for professionals looking to advance their careers or make a successful career transition. This is particularly relevant for athletes, first responders, mid-career professionals, lawyers, and doctors who are contemplating a change in their career paths. Building a strong network within your current field can open doors to new opportunities, provide valuable insights, and help you stay ahead of the game.

First and foremost, it's important to recognize the power of networking and the potential it holds. Your existing network may include colleagues, mentors, industry experts, and even friends and family members who can offer guidance or introduce you to key contacts. By expanding and nurturing these relationships, you can tap into a wealth of knowledge and experience that can prove invaluable in your career journey.

One effective way to expand your network within your current field is by attending industry conferences, seminars, and workshops. These events provide a platform for professionals to connect, share ideas, and build relationships. Take advantage of such opportunities to engage in meaningful conversations, participate in panel discussions, and exchange contact information with like-minded individuals. Remember, networking is a two-way street, so be sure to offer your own expertise and support to others as well.

Online platforms have revolutionized the way we connect and network. Utilize professional networking websites such as LinkedIn to build and enhance your digital network. Join industry-specific groups, engage in discussions, and reach out to individuals with similar interests or career goals. Virtual networking provides a unique platform to connect with professionals across the globe, regardless of geographical constraints.

Don't underestimate the power of informational interviews. Reach out to professionals within your field and request an opportunity to learn more about their experiences and gain insights into their career paths. These conversations can provide valuable guidance, expand your knowledge of potential career opportunities, and potentially lead to job opportunities down the line.

Don't forget the importance of nurturing existing relationships. Stay in touch with former colleagues, mentors, or supervisors by sending occasional updates, offering support, or simply catching up over a cup of coffee. These connections may prove to be invaluable in the future as they can provide referrals and recommendations or even be potential employers themselves.

Expanding your network within your current field is crucial for athletes, first responders, mid-career professionals, lawyers, and doctors looking to change their career paths. By attending industry events, utilizing online platforms, conducting informational interviews, and nurturing existing relationships, you can create a strong network that will support your career aspirations and help you navigate through any career transition successfully. Remember, networking is an ongoing process, so make it a priority and invest time and effort into building and maintaining meaningful connections within your industry.

Reaching out to Industry Professionals in Your Desired Career Path

Networking and building connections with industry professionals can be a crucial step in transitioning to a new career path. Whether you are an athlete looking to explore new opportunities, a first responder considering a career change, a mid-career professional seeking a fresh start, or even a lawyer or doctor longing for a different path, connecting with the right people can open doors and provide valuable insights.

One of the first steps in reaching out to industry professionals is identifying individuals who align with your desired career path. Research professional associations, online forums, and social media groups related to your target industry. Seek out individuals who have successfully made a similar transition and have valuable experience and knowledge to share. Look for opportunities to attend industry conferences, seminars, or workshops where you can connect with professionals face-to-face.

Once you have identified potential contacts, it's essential to approach them respectfully and professionally. Craft a well-thought-out introduction letter or email that explains your background, career goals, and why you are interested in connecting with them specifically. Highlight any relevant skills, experiences, or accomplishments that may grab their attention. Remember, industry professionals are more likely to respond if they see genuine interest and effort on your part.

When connecting with industry professionals, it's essential to be prepared and respectful of their time. Before reaching out, conduct thorough research on their background, work, and achievements. This will not only show your genuine interest but also help you craft meaningful questions and conversation topics. Be open-minded and willing to learn from their experiences and insights. Consider requesting an informational interview or a mentorship opportunity to build a relationship further.

Leveraging social media platforms such as LinkedIn can be an effective way to connect with industry professionals. Join relevant groups, participate in discussions, and engage with their content. By demonstrating your knowledge and passion for the industry, you may catch the attention of professionals who can guide you on your career transition journey.

Building relationships with industry professionals takes time and effort. It's crucial to maintain ongoing communication, express gratitude for their time and advice, and provide updates on your progress. Networking is a two-way street, so be prepared to offer support or assistance to professionals in return whenever possible.

Reaching out to industry professionals in your desired career path is a vital step in successfully transitioning to a new field. By networking, connecting, and learning from experienced individuals, you can gain valuable insights, open doors to new opportunities, and accelerate your career change journey.

Utilizing Social Media and Networking Events

Utilizing Social Media and Networking Events - Expanding Your Horizons and Career Opportunities

In today's rapidly evolving job market, the power of social media and networking events cannot be underestimated when it comes to successfully transitioning careers. Whether you are an athlete looking to explore new paths, a first responder seeking a change, a mid-career professional ready for new challenges, or even a lawyer or doctor contemplating a different direction, harnessing the potential of social media platforms and networking events can open up a world of opportunities.

Social media platforms like LinkedIn, Twitter, and Facebook have become invaluable tools for professional networking and career exploration. By creating a solid online presence, you can showcase your skills, experience, and aspirations to a broad audience. Connect with professionals in your desired field, join relevant groups and discussions, and share industry-related content to demonstrate your knowledge and passion. Engaging with influential figures and participating in conversations will not only expand your network but also expose you to potential job openings and career pathways you may not have considered before.

Attending networking events plays a crucial role in career transitions. These events provide a unique opportunity to meet industry professionals face-to-face, build relationships, and gain insights into specific career paths.

Seek out industry-specific conferences, seminars, and workshops where you can connect with like-minded individuals and hear from successful professionals who have made similar career transitions. Don't be afraid to approach speakers and attendees, introduce yourself, and share your career aspirations. The connections you make at these events can lead to mentorship opportunities, job referrals, or even partnerships for entrepreneurial ventures.

When utilizing social media and attending networking events, it is essential to be proactive and strategic. Research the attendees and speakers beforehand, identify specific individuals you would like to connect with and prepare thoughtful questions or conversation starters. Remember to follow up after the event, whether through LinkedIn or email, to express your gratitude and maintain the connection.

Social media and networking events have become indispensable resources for career changers across various professions. By utilizing these platforms effectively, athletes, first responders, mid-career professionals, lawyers, and doctors can expand their horizons, find new career paths, and connect with professionals who can offer guidance and support. Embrace the power of social media and networking events to navigate your career transition successfully and create exciting opportunities for your future.

Chapter 7 – Crafting a Compelling Resume and Cover Letter

Showcasing Transferable Skills and Accomplishments

In today's fast-paced and ever-changing professional landscape, the ability to change career paths has become a necessity rather than a luxury. Whether you are an athlete, a first responder, a mid-career professional, a lawyer, or a doctor, the need to adapt and transition into a new field is becoming increasingly common. However, the key to successfully making this transition is effectively showcasing your transferable skills and accomplishments.

One of the main challenges athletes, first responders, mid-career professionals, lawyers, and doctors face when changing career paths is convincing potential employers that their skills are applicable and valuable in a different industry. This subchapter aims to guide you through the process of identifying, highlighting, and effectively communicating your transferable skills and accomplishments to potential employers.

First and foremost, it is essential to recognize the unique set of skills you have developed throughout your career.

Athletes possess qualities such as discipline, teamwork, leadership, and the ability to perform under pressure. First responders have honed skills like quick decision-making, problem-solving, and remaining calm in high-stress situations. Mid-career professionals bring a wealth of experience, adaptability, and a proven track record of success. Lawyers and doctors have developed exceptional analytical skills, attention to detail, and the ability to handle complex information. Identifying these transferable skills is the first step towards showcasing them effectively.

Once you have identified your transferable skills, the next step is to highlight your accomplishments. This could include specific achievements, awards, certifications, or even successful projects you have completed. By showcasing your accomplishments, you provide tangible evidence of your capabilities and demonstrate how your skills have translated into real-world results.

To effectively communicate your transferable skills and accomplishments, it is crucial to tailor your resume, cover letter, and interview responses to the specific requirements of the new industry you are targeting. Use language that resonates with the sector and incorporates relevant keywords to capture the attention of potential employers. Additionally, leverage your professional network and consider seeking mentorship or guidance from individuals who have successfully transitioned into a new field.

Changing career paths can be a daunting task, but by effectively showcasing your transferable skills and accomplishments, you can position yourself as a valuable asset in any industry. This subchapter has provided you with the necessary guidance to identify, highlight, and communicate your skills and achievements to potential employers. Remember, your unique experiences and accomplishments are what set you apart, and with the right approach, you can successfully navigate a career transition and embark on a fulfilling new path.

Tailoring Your Resume for Different Job Applications

In today's competitive job market, it is essential to present yourself as the best candidate for the job. One way to do this is by tailoring your resume for different job applications. Whether you are an athlete, first responder, mid-career professional, lawyer, or doctor looking to change career paths, this subchapter will guide you through the process step-by-step.

1. Identify your transferable skills - Begin by understanding your unique skill set and identifying the skills that are transferable to your desired career path. For athletes, this could include teamwork, discipline, and leadership, while first responders may possess excellent problem-solving and communication skills.

2. Research your target industry - Next, research the industry you are interested in. Understand the key skills and qualifications employers are seeking. Look for job descriptions and requirements to gain insights into the language and terminologies used in the industry.

3. Customize your resume - Once you have identified your transferable skills and researched the industry, it's time to customize your resume. Tailor your resume to highlight the skills and experiences that align with the job requirements. Use industry-specific keywords and phrases to grab the attention of hiring managers.

4. Focus on achievements - When changing career paths, it's crucial to showcase your accomplishments and achievements. Highlight any relevant accomplishments that demonstrate your ability to succeed in the new field. This could include awards, certifications, or notable projects you have worked on.

5. Address gaps and challenges - Changing career paths may come with its own set of challenges. Be prepared to address any gaps or challenges in your resume. If you lack specific qualifications, focus on transferable skills or highlight any relevant training or certifications you have obtained.

6. Seek professional assistance - If you find the process overwhelming, consider seeking professional assistance. Career coaches or resume writers can provide valuable guidance and help you create a compelling resume tailored to your target industry.

By tailoring your resume for different job applications, you increase your chances of standing out from the competition and securing your desired career path. Remember to continuously update and refine your resume as you gain new skills and experiences. With the right approach and a well-crafted resume, you can successfully navigate your career transition.

Writing an Engaging Cover Letter

In today's competitive job market, a well-crafted cover letter can be the key to landing your dream job and successfully transitioning into a new career path. Whether you are an athlete, first responder, mid-career professional, lawyer, or doctor, mastering the art of writing an engaging cover letter is essential to standing out from the crowd. This subchapter will guide you through the process of creating a cover letter that captivates employers and highlights your unique qualifications.

1. Understanding the Purpose -

Before diving into the writing process, it's crucial to understand the purpose of a cover letter. It serves as your introduction to potential employers, giving you an opportunity to showcase your skills, experience, and passion. It should complement your resume by providing more context and emphasizing why you are the perfect candidate for the position.

2. Customizing for Career Transition -

When changing career paths, it's essential to address any potential concerns employers may have. Focus on transferable skills and experiences that relate to the desired role. Highlight relevant accomplishments and abilities that demonstrate your adaptability and willingness to learn.

3. Captivating Opening -

Start your cover letter with an attention-grabbing opening that immediately captures the reader's interest. Consider incorporating a personal anecdote, a thought-provoking question, or a compelling statistic related to the industry or role.

4. Showcasing Value -

Use the body of the cover letter to highlight your value proposition. Clearly articulate how your skills, experience, and expertise make you an asset to the organization.

5. Researching the Company -

Demonstrate your genuine interest and knowledge of the company by conducting thorough research. Incorporate relevant details about the organization's values, mission, recent achievements, or projects in your cover letter. This shows your dedication and enthusiasm for joining their team.

6. Authenticity and Professionalism -

Strike a balance between showcasing your personality and maintaining professionalism. Use a conversational yet respectful tone, and ensure your writing is error-free and well-structured. Be authentic and let your passion for the new career path shine through.

7. Call to Action -

Conclude your cover letter with a solid and straightforward call to action. Express your enthusiasm for the opportunity to discuss your qualifications further in an interview and provide your contact information.

Remember, writing an engaging cover letter is an ongoing process that requires refinement and customization for each job application. By following these guidelines and tailoring your cover letter to suit your career transition, you will significantly increase your chances of securing interviews and successfully changing career paths.

Chapter 8 – Mastering the Job Search Process

Utilizing Job Search Websites and Platforms

In today's fast-paced and interconnected world, the internet has become an invaluable resource for job seekers from all walks of life. Athletes, first responders, mid-career professionals, lawyers, and doctors can all benefit significantly from utilizing job search websites and platforms to explore new career paths and find exciting opportunities. This subchapter will guide you through the process of effectively using these online tools to navigate your career transition successfully.

First and foremost, it's essential to understand the different types of job search websites and platforms available to you. There are general job boards, such as Indeed, LinkedIn, and Glassdoor, which offer a wide range of job listings across various industries. These platforms are excellent starting points for exploring different career options and understanding the market demand for your skills and experience.

However, for athletes, first responders, and professionals in specialized fields like law and medicine, niche job boards can provide even more tailored opportunities. Websites like TeamWork Online, Firefighter Jobs, and Medscape Careers specifically cater to these industries, allowing you to find job openings that align with your unique background.

Once you have identified the relevant job search websites and platforms, it's crucial to optimize your profile and tailor your resume for maximum impact. Take the time to craft a compelling summary that highlights your critical skills, experiences, and achievements. Utilize keywords and industry-specific terminology to increase your visibility to potential employers.

Networking is another critical aspect of utilizing job search websites and platforms effectively. Connect with professionals in your desired field, join industry-specific groups, and participate in discussions to expand your network. Many platforms offer messaging features that allow you to reach out directly to hiring managers or industry experts, so don't hesitate to make connections and seek advice.

Be proactive in your job search. Set up email alerts or notifications for new job postings that match your criteria. Regularly update your profile and resume to showcase your most recent accomplishments. Consistency and persistence are key when utilizing job search websites and platforms.

Job search websites and platforms are powerful tools that athletes, first responders, mid-career professionals, lawyers, and doctors can leverage when changing career paths.

Leveraging Recruitment Agencies and Headhunters

In today's ever-evolving job market, changing career paths can be a daunting task. Whether you're an athlete transitioning out of professional sports, a first responder looking to explore new opportunities, a mid-career professional seeking a change, or even a lawyer or doctor considering a shift in your career trajectory, understanding how to leverage recruitment agencies effectively and headhunters can be a game-changer.

Recruitment agencies and headhunters are professionals who specialize in connecting talented individuals with job opportunities that align with their skills, experience, and aspirations. These experts have a deep understanding of various industries and can provide invaluable guidance and support throughout the career transition process.

One of the key benefits of partnering with recruitment agencies and headhunters is their extensive network of contacts within the industry. They have established relationships with hiring managers, HR professionals, and key decision-makers, giving them access to a hidden job market that may not be advertised publicly. By tapping into this network, you can unlock a multitude of career opportunities that may not be accessible through traditional job search methods.

Moreover, recruitment agencies and headhunters possess a wealth of knowledge about market trends, industry demands, and the skills that are currently in high demand. They can provide you with valuable insights into the skills and experience you need to develop or highlight to stand out in your desired field. This knowledge can help you make informed decisions about additional education or training programs to enhance your marketability and increase your chances of securing your dream job.

These professionals are skilled in resume writing, interview preparation, and negotiation tactics. They can help you craft a compelling resume and cover letter that highlight your transferable skills and experiences, making you a strong candidate in the eyes of potential employers. They can also coach you on interview techniques, ensuring you present yourself confidently and effectively during the hiring process. Furthermore, they can assist you in negotiating job offers, ensuring you receive fair compensation and benefits in your new role.

By leveraging the expertise of recruitment agencies and headhunters, athletes, first responders, mid-career professionals, lawyers, and doctors can navigate the complexities of changing career paths more effectively. These professionals can provide valuable guidance, access to a hidden job market, industry insights, and expert support to help you achieve a successful career transition.

Navigating the Hidden Job Market

In today's competitive job market, finding new career opportunities can be challenging, especially for athletes, first responders, mid-career professionals, lawyers, and doctors. Traditional job search methods like submitting resumes online or attending job fairs may not always yield the desired results. This is where understanding and navigating the hidden job market becomes crucial.

What is the hidden job market? It refers to job openings that are not publicly advertised or posted, making them less accessible to the general public. These opportunities often arise through networking, referrals, and personal connections. To successfully tap into this hidden job market and make a career transition, athletes, first responders, mid-career professionals, lawyers, and doctors must follow a strategic approach.

Building a strong professional network is essential. Contact colleagues, former teammates, mentors, and industry professionals who can offer guidance and support. Attend industry-specific events, conferences, and seminars to meet potential employers and expand your network. By establishing these connections, you increase your chances of learning about hidden job opportunities before they are publicly announced.

Additionally, consider working with a career coach or mentor specializing in career transitions. These professionals can provide valuable insights, help you identify transferable skills, and guide you through the process of changing career paths. They can also assist in creating a compelling resume and cover letter that highlights your strengths and showcases your potential to employers in your desired field.

Utilizing online platforms and professional networking websites can also be beneficial. Create a robust online presence by updating your LinkedIn profile, sharing relevant industry content, and engaging with others in your field. Many hidden job opportunities are discovered through online networking, so it's important to participate in discussions and showcase your expertise actively.

Don't underestimate the power of informational interviews. Contact professionals in your desired field and request a casual meeting to gather information about their career paths and industry insights. Not only will this help you gain valuable knowledge, but it may also open doors to hidden job opportunities or potential referrals.

Chapter 9 – Acing Interviews and Negotiating Job Offers

Preparing for Different Types of Interviews

In the journey of changing career paths, one of the most crucial steps is the interview process. Whether you are an athlete, a first responder, a mid-career professional, a lawyer, or a doctor, being well-prepared for different types of interviews is essential. This subchapter will equip you with the necessary knowledge and strategies to excel in any interview scenario.

1. Research, Research, Research - Before any interview, it is imperative to research the company or organization you are applying to thoroughly. Understand their mission, values, goals, and recent achievements. This will not only demonstrate your genuine interest but also help you align your skills and experiences with their requirements.

2. Tailor Your Resume - As you transition into a new career, it is vital to tailor your resume to highlight relevant skills and experiences. Emphasize transferable skills that can be applied to the new role and showcase any relevant certifications or training you have obtained.

3. Practice Common Interview Questions - Prepare for common interview questions such as "Tell me about yourself," "Why do you want to work here?" and "What are your strengths and weaknesses?" Practice crafting concise and compelling responses that showcase your unique qualities and demonstrate how they align with the position you are applying for.

4. Behavioral Interviews - Many organizations conduct behavioral interviews to assess how candidates handle specific situations. Prepare by identifying examples from your past experiences that highlight your problem-solving abilities, leadership skills, teamwork, and adaptability. Structure your answers using the STAR method (Situation, Task, Action, Result) to provide a comprehensive response.

5. Technical Interviews - Depending on the career path you choose, you may encounter technical interviews that assess your knowledge and skills in a particular field. Prepare by revisiting relevant concepts, practicing problem-solving exercises, and seeking guidance from professionals already working in the field.

6. Role-Play - Consider conducting mock interviews with a friend or coach to simulate real interview situations. This will help you refine your communication skills, build confidence, and identify areas for improvement.

7. Follow-Up - After each interview, send a personalized thank-you email or note to express your gratitude for the opportunity. This small gesture will leave a lasting impression on the interviewers and showcase your professionalism.

Preparing for different types of interviews is a critical aspect of successfully changing career paths. By conducting thorough research, tailoring your resume, practicing common and behavioral interview questions, preparing for technical interviews, role-playing, and following up, you will be well-equipped to face any interview scenario with confidence and competence. Remember, every interview is an opportunity to showcase your unique skills, experiences, and potential to excel in your new career.

Answering Common Interview Questions

When it comes to changing career paths, one of the most crucial steps is successfully navigating the interview process. Interviews can be nerve-wracking, especially if you are transitioning from one field to another. However, with the right preparation and guidance, you can confidently tackle any interview and showcase your skills and potential to potential employers. In this subchapter, we will discuss some of the most common interview questions and provide you with tips and strategies to help you craft impressive responses.

1. "Tell me about yourself."

This question is often used as an icebreaker and an opportunity for you to provide a brief overview of your background. Focus on your transferable skills, relevant experiences, and your passion for the new career path. Highlight any accomplishments or experiences that demonstrate your ability to adapt and succeed in new environments.

2. "Why are you interested in this career?"

This question lets you showcase your enthusiasm and commitment to the new career path. Discuss how your skills and experiences align with the role's demands and how your previous career has prepared you for this transition. Be specific about what attracts you to this new field and how you plan to contribute and grow in it.

3. "What are your strengths and weaknesses?"

Highlight your strengths by aligning them with the requirements of the new career. Discuss how your previous experiences have developed these strengths and how they will benefit your future endeavors. When addressing weaknesses, focus on areas where you have taken steps to improve and demonstrate your ability to learn from challenges.

4. "Describe a difficult situation you faced at work and how you resolved it."

Use this question as an opportunity to showcase your problem-solving skills and ability to handle adversity. Discuss a specific situation where you encountered a challenge, how you analyzed it, and the steps you took to resolve it. Highlight any positive outcomes or lessons learned from this experience.

5. "Where do you see yourself in five years?"

Demonstrate your long-term commitment to the new career path by discussing your goals and aspirations. Talk about the skills you want to develop, the impact you hope to make, and the potential growth opportunities you see within the new field. Emphasize your dedication and willingness to invest in your professional development.

By familiarizing yourself with these typical interview questions and preparing thoughtful and tailored responses, you can approach your career transition interviews with confidence. Remember, the key is to showcase your transferable skills, passion for the new career, and ability to adapt and learn. With thorough preparation and practice, you can successfully navigate any interview and make a compelling case for your career change.

Negotiating Salary, Benefits, and Work–Life Balance

When considering a career transition, negotiating salary, benefits, and work-life balance are crucial aspects that must be thoroughly assessed. Whether you are an athlete looking to transition into a new field, a first responder seeking a different career path, a mid-career professional considering a change, or even a lawyer or doctor contemplating a shift in focus, understanding the intricacies of these negotiations can significantly impact your success and satisfaction in your new career.

It is essential to research the salary range and benefits within your desired industry or field. Online resources, industry reports, and networking can provide valuable insights into the average compensation package for professionals in similar roles. Armed with this knowledge, you can confidently enter negotiations and advocate for a fair and competitive salary.

Benefits are pivotal in overall job satisfaction and work-life balance. Consider the importance of health insurance, retirement plans, paid time off, and other perks that align with your personal and professional goals. During negotiations, be prepared to discuss these benefits and negotiate for ones that are meaningful to you. Understanding the value of these benefits will allow you to assess the overall compensation package and make informed decisions.

Work-life balance is increasingly recognized as a vital component of a fulfilling career. Assess your personal priorities and determine what balance means to you. Are flexible work hours or remote work options essential? Will you have the opportunity to pursue personal interests outside of work? Negotiating for a work-life balance that aligns with your needs and aspirations is critical for long-term career satisfaction and overall well-being.

To successfully negotiate salary, benefits, and work-life balance, it is essential to develop strong communication and negotiation skills. Practice articulating your value proposition, highlighting your unique skills and experiences that make you a valuable asset to any organization. Understand your worth and be confident in expressing it.

Negotiations are not a one-time event. As your career progresses, continue to reassess your compensation package and advocate for adjustments that reflect your growth and contributions.

Negotiating salary, benefits, and work-life balance is a crucial step in any career transition. Athletes, first responders, mid-career professionals, lawyers, and doctors must be equipped with the knowledge and skills to advocate for themselves effectively. By understanding industry standards, valuing benefits, prioritizing work-life balance, and developing strong negotiation skills, you can ensure a successful transition and a fulfilling new career path.

Chapter 10 – Thriving in Your New Career

Onboarding and Adjusting to a New Work Environment

Transitioning into a new career can be both exciting and overwhelming. Whether you are an athlete, a first responder, a mid-career professional, a lawyer, or a doctor, the process of changing career paths requires careful planning and adjustment to a new work environment. In this subchapter, we will explore the essential strategies and tips to help you navigate this critical phase of your professional journey.

First and foremost, it is crucial to recognize that adjusting to a new work environment takes time. Just as athletes undergo rigorous training to excel in their sport, professionals must invest time and effort into understanding the dynamics, culture, and expectations of their new workplace. Patience and a growth mindset are essential during this transition period.

To smoothly integrate into your new work environment, establish a strong foundation by building relationships with your colleagues. Engage in open communication, seek opportunities to collaborate, and actively participate in team activities. Networking within your organization can provide invaluable support and guidance as you navigate your new career path.

Take the initiative to learn about the industry and the specific role you are transitioning into. Stay up to date with industry trends, attend relevant conferences or workshops, and seek mentorship from experienced professionals. This proactive approach will not only deepen your knowledge but also demonstrate your commitment to your new career.

Embrace the learning curve that comes with changing career paths. Recognize that you may need to acquire new skills or enhance existing ones to excel in your new role. Seek out training programs, certifications, or online courses that can help you bridge any skill gaps. By investing in your professional development, you will build confidence and increase your chances of success.

Remember to take care of yourself during this transition. Changing career paths can be mentally and emotionally demanding. Prioritize self-care activities such as exercise, mindfulness, and maintaining a healthy work-life balance. Surround yourself with a support system that understands and supports your career transition.

Navigating a career transition requires careful onboarding and adjustment to a new work environment. By developing relationships, learning about the industry, embracing the learning curve, and taking care of yourself, you can successfully transition into a new career path. Remember, change is an opportunity for growth, and with the right mindset and strategies, you can thrive in your new journey.

Building Rapport with Colleagues and Superiors

In today's competitive job market, building strong relationships with colleagues and superiors is essential for career success. Whether you are an athlete transitioning into a new career, a first responder looking to change career paths, a mid-career professional seeking a fresh start, or a lawyer or doctor exploring new opportunities, the ability to establish rapport with others is crucial. This subchapter aims to provide you with practical strategies and tips to build rapport in your new professional environment effectively.

It is crucial to cultivate a positive attitude and approachability. Smile, maintain open body language, and be genuine in your interactions. Displaying a positive demeanor creates an inviting atmosphere and makes it easier for others to approach you. Actively listen to your colleagues and superiors, showing interest in their ideas, opinions, and experiences. This not only helps in building rapport but also enables you to learn from their expertise and gain valuable insights.

Another key aspect of building rapport is effective communication. Pay attention to your verbal and non-verbal cues, ensuring they convey respect and professionalism. Be mindful of your tone and choice of words, maintaining a balance between assertiveness and diplomacy. Moreover, be aware of cultural differences and adapt your communication style accordingly, fostering an inclusive and harmonious work environment.

Invest time in getting to know your colleagues and superiors outside of work-related conversations. Engage in informal interactions such as team-building activities, networking events, or simply grabbing a coffee together. These opportunities allow for building personal connections and understanding each other's interests and values.

Showcasing your expertise and willingness to learn will help you gain the respect and trust of your colleagues and superiors. Be proactive in seeking feedback and guidance, demonstrating your commitment to personal and professional growth. This not only enhances your skills but also establishes you as a valuable team member.

Be mindful of office politics and navigate them with diplomacy. Avoid taking sides in conflicts and maintain a neutral stance. Focus on building relationships based on trust and respect rather than engaging in gossip or negative discussions.

Building rapport with colleagues and superiors is crucial when transitioning into a new career path. By cultivating a positive attitude, effective communication, active listening, investing in personal connections, showcasing expertise, and navigating office politics with diplomacy, you can establish strong relationships that contribute to your professional success and overall job satisfaction.

Continuously Learning and Growing in Your New Role

In today's fast-paced and ever-evolving world, the ability to adapt and grow is essential for success in any career. Whether you are an athlete transitioning into a new profession, a first responder looking for a change, a mid-career professional seeking new challenges, or even a lawyer or doctor considering a career switch, the key to a successful career transition lies in continuously learning and growing in your new role.

Embrace a Growth Mindset

One of the first steps in this journey is to adopt a growth mindset. Understand that your new career path will demand new skills and knowledge. Embracing the belief that you can develop and improve these skills through dedication and effort is crucial. View challenges as opportunities for growth, and approach them with a positive and open mindset.

Seek Opportunities for Learning

To expand your expertise and knowledge in your new field, actively seek out learning opportunities. Attend conferences, workshops, and seminars related to your new profession. Engage in online courses, webinars, or podcasts that offer insights and updates on industry trends. Take advantage of professional development programs and mentorship opportunities, or consider returning to school to acquire additional qualifications.

Network and Collaborate

Building a solid professional network is vital when changing career paths. Connect with individuals in your new field who can offer guidance and share valuable insights. Attend industry events, join relevant associations, and participate in online communities to expand your network. Collaborate with others in your field to exchange ideas, learn from their experiences, and gain exposure to different perspectives.

Stay Informed and Stay Ahead

To thrive in your new role, it is essential to stay informed about the latest developments in your industry. Subscribe to industry newsletters, follow influential thought leaders and organizations on social media, and read books and articles related to your field. Keep an eye on emerging trends and technologies, and continuously update your skills to stay ahead of the curve.

Embrace Challenges and Feedback

Transitioning to a new career can be challenging, but it is through these challenges that you grow and develop. Embrace the discomfort that comes with stepping out of your comfort zone and see it as an opportunity for personal and professional growth. Seek feedback from mentors, colleagues, and supervisors to identify areas for improvement and actively work on enhancing your skills.

As athletes, first responders, mid-career professionals, lawyers, or doctors, you have already demonstrated resilience, dedication, and a strong work ethic. By continuously learning and growing in your new role, you can leverage these qualities to navigate career transitions successfully and achieve long-term fulfillment and success. Remember, the journey to a new career path is about embracing change, embracing growth, and embracing the opportunity to become the best version of yourself.

Chapter 11 – Overcoming Challenges and Staying Resilient

Dealing with Imposter Syndrome and Self-Doubt

Imposter Syndrome and self-doubt are common challenges that many individuals face when considering a career transition. Whether you are an athlete, a first responder, a mid-career professional, a lawyer, or a doctor, these feelings can often hinder your progress and prevent you from pursuing your true passions. In this subchapter, we will explore practical strategies to tackle Imposter Syndrome and overcome self-doubt, empowering you to confidently navigate your journey of changing career paths.

It is essential to recognize that Imposter Syndrome is a common phenomenon experienced by high-achieving individuals. It involves feeling like a fraud despite evidence of competence and accomplishments. By understanding that you are not alone in these feelings, you can begin to challenge the negative thoughts and beliefs associated with Imposter Syndrome.

One effective strategy to combat Imposter Syndrome is to reframe your mindset. Start by acknowledging your accomplishments, skills, and experiences. Remind yourself of the successes you have achieved throughout your career, whether it be on the field, in the courtroom, or in the operating room. By focusing on your strengths and unique qualities, you can build confidence and diminish feelings of self-doubt.

Another powerful tool is seeking support from others who have gone through similar career transitions. Connecting with mentors, coaches, or individuals who have successfully navigated a similar path can provide invaluable guidance and reassurance. They can offer insights, share their own experiences, and help you develop a roadmap for success.

Additionally, practicing self-care is crucial in combating Imposter Syndrome and self-doubt. Engage in activities that bring you joy, reduce stress, and promote a healthy work-life balance. This could include exercise, meditation, spending time with loved ones, or pursuing hobbies. Taking care of your physical and mental well-being will enhance your self-confidence and overall resilience.

Finally, embrace the growth mindset. Understand that change and learning are part of the process when embarking on a new career path. Embrace challenges as opportunities for growth and view failures as valuable learning experiences.

Imposter Syndrome and self-doubt can be significant barriers when changing career paths, but they are not insurmountable. By reframing your mindset, seeking support from others, practicing self-care, and embracing a growth mindset, you can overcome these challenges and confidently make your transition. Remember, you have the skills, experiences, and unique qualities necessary to succeed in any career you choose.

Managing Setbacks and Rejections

In the journey of changing career paths, setbacks and rejections are inevitable. Whether you are an athlete, a first responder, a mid-career professional, a lawyer, or a doctor, transitioning into a new field can be challenging and filled with obstacles. However, it is how you manage these setbacks and rejections that will determine your success in this endeavor.

One of the first steps in managing setbacks is to embrace the mindset of resilience. Understand that setbacks are not indicators of failure but rather opportunities for growth and learning. Athletes are familiar with setbacks in their sports careers, but this mindset can be applied to any profession. By viewing setbacks as stepping stones rather than stumbling blocks, you can maintain a positive outlook and persevere through difficult times.

Another crucial aspect of managing setbacks and rejections is maintaining a solid support system. Surround yourself with individuals who believe in your potential and can offer guidance and encouragement during challenging times. Seek out mentors who have successfully navigated career transitions and learn from their experiences. Their insights can provide valuable insights and help you develop strategies for overcoming setbacks and rejections.

When faced with rejection, it is important to remember that it is not a reflection of your worth or abilities. Rejections are often subjective and can be influenced by various factors beyond your control. Instead of dwelling on the rejection, focus on constructive feedback and areas for improvement. Use this feedback as fuel to enhance your skills and refine your approach.

Developing a growth mindset can greatly aid in managing setbacks and rejections. Embrace the idea that your abilities and talents can be developed through dedication and hard work. By adopting a growth mindset, you can view setbacks as opportunities to learn and improve rather than as roadblocks.

Be adaptable and willing to explore new opportunities. Changing career paths often involves stepping outside of your comfort zone. Embrace the unknown and be open to new experiences and challenges. This flexibility will allow you to navigate setbacks and rejections with grace.

Managing setbacks and rejections is an integral part of any career transition, whether you are an athlete, a first responder, a mid-career professional, a lawyer, or a doctor. By embracing resilience, building a solid support system, maintaining a growth mindset, and staying adaptable, you can overcome obstacles and successfully navigate a new career path. Remember, setbacks are not failures but opportunities for growth and, ultimately, success.

Maintaining Work–Life Balance in a New Career

In today's fast-paced world, achieving a work-life balance is a challenge that many individuals face, especially when transitioning into a new career. Whether you are an athlete, a first responder, a mid-career professional, a lawyer, or a doctor, balancing your personal and professional life remains vital for your overall well-being and success. This subchapter aims to provide you with essential strategies and practical tips to help you maintain a healthy work-life balance during your career transition.

One of the first steps in achieving work-life balance is setting clear boundaries between work and personal life. As you embark on a new career path, it can be tempting to immerse yourself entirely in your work, neglecting other aspects of your life. However, it is crucial to establish boundaries to ensure that your personal relationships, hobbies, and self-care routines are not compromised. Set specific working hours and allocate dedicated time for family, friends, and leisure activities. This will help you create a structured routine and prioritize your personal life alongside your professional commitments.

Another critical aspect of maintaining a work-life balance is learning to delegate and ask for support. As you transition into a new career, it is natural to feel overwhelmed and take on more responsibilities. However, recognizing your limitations and seeking assistance when needed is crucial for preventing burnout and maintaining a healthy balance. Delegate tasks, both at work and at home, to trusted colleagues, family members, or professionals, allowing you to focus on what truly matters to you.

Additionally, it is essential to take care of your physical and mental well-being during this career transition. Engage in regular exercise, practice mindfulness techniques, and prioritize self-care activities such as getting enough sleep, eating healthy, and taking breaks when needed. By nurturing your overall well-being, you will be better equipped to handle the challenges of your new career.

Remember that achieving work-life balance is an ongoing process. As you progress in your new career and face new challenges, it is essential to reassess your priorities and make any necessary adjustments regularly. Be flexible and open to change, as your needs and circumstances may evolve over time.

Maintaining a work-life balance during a career transition is crucial for athletes, first responders, mid-career professionals, lawyers, and doctors alike. By setting boundaries, delegating tasks, prioritizing self-care, and being adaptable, you can successfully navigate your new career path while still enjoying a fulfilling personal life. Remember, achieving work-life balance is an ongoing journey, and with the right strategies and mindset, you can find harmony between your personal and professional pursuits.

Chapter 12 – Continuing Professional Development and Growth

Seeking Mentorship and Coaching Opportunities

In the journey of changing career paths, seeking mentorship and coaching opportunities can be a game-changer. Whether you are an athlete, first responder, mid-career professional, lawyer, or doctor, the guidance and support from experienced mentors and coaches can provide invaluable insights and propel you toward success in your new career.

Mentorship and coaching are essential components of any successful career transition. They offer a unique opportunity to learn from someone who has already walked the path you are about to embark on. Mentors can provide guidance, share their experiences, and provide advice on overcoming challenges. Their wisdom and expertise can help you avoid common pitfalls and accelerate your learning curve.

Finding the right mentor or coach begins with self-reflection. Take the time to identify your career goals, strengths, and areas for improvement. This self-awareness will help you narrow down the specific expertise you seek in a mentor or coach. Whether you are looking for industry-specific guidance or assistance with personal development, having a clear vision of your needs will ensure you find the right fit.

There are various avenues to explore when seeking mentorship and coaching opportunities. Professional associations, alumni networks, and online platforms dedicated to connecting mentors and mentees are great places to start. Attend networking events or join online communities to expand your professional network and increase your chances of finding a suitable mentor or coach.

When approaching potential mentors or coaches, it is essential to be respectful and considerate of their time. Craft a well-thought-out message explaining why you believe they would be a valuable mentor or coach for you. Highlight your goals, aspirations, and how their expertise aligns with your career transition. Remember, mentors and coaches are likelier to invest their time in individuals who demonstrate commitment and dedication.

Once you have established a mentor or coach relationship, make the most of the opportunity. Be open to feedback and constructive criticism, as this will help you grow and develop. Set clear goals with your mentor or coach and regularly assess your progress. Leverage their expertise to expand knowledge and skill set, and don't hesitate to ask for help.

Seeking mentorship and coaching opportunities can be a transformative experience in your career transition journey. Embrace the wisdom and guidance of experienced professionals, and watch as they help you navigate the challenges and opportunities that lie ahead. Remember, success is not achieved alone, and with the right mentor or coach by your side, you can confidently embrace your new career path.

Pursuing Additional Training and Certifications

In today's rapidly changing job market, the importance of continuous learning and professional development cannot be overstated. Whether you are an athlete looking to transition into a new career, a first responder seeking a change of pace, a mid-career professional yearning for growth, or even a lawyer or doctor considering a shift in your chosen path, acquiring additional training and certifications can significantly enhance your career prospects. This subchapter will guide you through the process of pursuing further education and certifications, providing you with a step-by-step approach to successfully changing career paths.

One of the first steps in pursuing additional training and certifications is to assess your current skills and identify the areas in which you need to expand your knowledge. This self-analysis will help you understand the gaps in your skillset and enable you to choose the right courses or certifications that align with your desired career path. It is crucial to select programs that are recognized and respected in your target industry to ensure your investment of time and resources pays off.

When considering further education, it's essential to evaluate the various learning options available. Traditional classroom-based courses, online programs, workshops, and mentorship opportunities are just a few examples. Each option has its advantages and disadvantages, so it's crucial to choose the one that suits your learning style, schedule, and budget.

Financing your additional training and certifications is another aspect to consider. Many organizations and institutions offer scholarships, grants, or financial aid programs designed explicitly for career transitioners. Additionally, you may explore employer-sponsored tuition reimbursement programs or consider taking out a loan if necessary. Careful financial planning will ensure that you can pursue the necessary education without undue burden.

Once you have identified the appropriate training and certification programs and secured the necessary funding, it is time to embark on your learning journey. Dedicate time and effort to immerse yourself in the courses fully, leveraging all available resources and support. Networking with industry professionals, joining relevant associations, and participating in workshops or conferences can further enhance your learning experience and expand your professional network.

Finally, always remember that acquiring additional training and certifications is not a one-time event but an ongoing process. Continuously seek opportunities to upgrade your skills, stay abreast of industry trends, and adapt to the ever-evolving job market. By investing in your professional development, you will position yourself as a competitive candidate and successfully navigate your career transition.

In conclusion, pursuing additional training and certifications is a crucial step towards changing career paths. By assessing your skills, selecting the right programs, securing funding, and fully engaging in the learning process, you can acquire the knowledge and qualifications necessary to thrive in your desired field. Remember, a commitment to lifelong learning is a crucial characteristic of successful career transitioners, athletes, first responders, mid-career professionals, lawyers, doctors, and individuals from all walks of life.

Staying Updated with Industry Trends and Best Practices

In today's fast-paced and ever-evolving world, staying updated with industry trends and best practices is crucial for individuals looking to transition into new career paths. Whether you are an athlete, a first responder, a mid-career professional, a lawyer, or a doctor, the ability to adapt and learn is essential in successfully changing your career path.

This subchapter of "The Playbook for Athlete Career Transitions - A Step-by-Step Guide" will provide you with valuable insights into how to stay updated with industry trends and best practices. By following these steps, you can ensure that you are always on top of your game and ready to tackle new challenges in your chosen field.

First and foremost, it is essential to develop a mindset of continuous learning. Embrace the idea that learning is a lifelong process and commit to staying curious and open-minded. Take advantage of various resources such as industry publications, online forums, podcasts, and webinars to gain knowledge about the latest trends and practices in your desired field.

Networking plays a crucial role in staying updated with industry trends. Connect with professionals in your industry through networking events, conferences, and online platforms like LinkedIn. Engage in conversations, ask questions, and seek advice from those who are already established in your desired field. This will not only help you stay updated but also provide you with valuable connections and potential career opportunities.

Consider joining professional associations and organizations related to your new career path. These groups often provide access to exclusive industry insights, webinars, conferences, and networking opportunities. By becoming a member, you can gain insights from industry leaders and stay updated with the latest trends and best practices.

Use online learning platforms and courses to acquire new skills and knowledge. Many websites offer courses on a wide range of topics, from project management to digital marketing, enabling you to enhance your expertise and stay updated with industry-specific practices.

Stay connected with your peers and colleagues. Engage in discussions, share ideas, and collaborate on projects. By fostering a community of like-minded professionals, you can collectively stay updated with industry trends, share best practices, and support each other in your career transitions.

Staying updated with industry trends and best practices is essential for individuals looking to change career paths. By maintaining a mindset of continuous learning, networking with professionals, joining professional associations, taking online courses, and staying connected with peers, you can ensure that you are always up-to-date and well-prepared for your new career journey. Remember, success lies in your ability to adapt and embrace change, and staying updated will undoubtedly give you a competitive edge in your chosen field.

Chapter 13 – Inspiring Success Stories and Lessons Learned

Athletes Who Successfully Transitioned to New Careers

In the fast-paced world of sports, athletes often find themselves at a crossroads when their playing days come to an end. However, there are those exceptional individuals who have not only gracefully transitioned to new careers but have excelled in them as well. This subchapter explores the inspiring stories of athletes who have successfully navigated the challenging path of career transition, offering valuable insights and guidance to athletes, first responders, mid-career professionals, lawyers, and doctors.

Transitioning to a new career can be a daunting task, especially for individuals who have dedicated their lives to a specific sport or profession. However, the stories of these extraordinary athletes serve as beacons of hope and motivation for those who find themselves at a similar career crossroads.

One such example is Michael Jordan, widely regarded as one of the greatest basketball players of all time. Following his retirement from professional basketball, Jordan redirected his focus towards entrepreneurship, becoming the owner of the Charlotte Hornets and establishing himself as a successful businessman. His story demonstrates the importance of leveraging one's skills, passion, and personal brand to forge a new career path.

Another remarkable story is that of Dara Torres, an Olympic swimmer who competed in five different Olympic Games. After retiring from swimming, Torres transitioned to a successful career as a motivational speaker, author, and fitness advocate. Her ability to leverage her athletic achievements and inspire others showcases the power of identifying transferable skills and finding a new purpose beyond the field or the pool.

But it's not just athletes who can find inspiration in these stories. First responders, mid-career professionals, lawyers, and doctors can also draw valuable lessons from these successful career transitions. The ability to identify transferable skills, develop a growth mindset, and embrace new opportunities are universal principles that can be applied to any career change.

This subchapter aims to provide practical guidance and actionable steps for individuals seeking to change career paths. It delves into the mindset required for a successful transition, the importance of personal branding, and strategies for identifying transferable skills. It also explores the potential challenges and roadblocks that may arise during the process and offers strategies for overcoming them.

By examining the journeys of athletes who have successfully transitioned to new careers, this subchapter equips athletes, first responders, mid-career professionals, lawyers, and doctors with the tools and inspiration they need to navigate their own career transitions. It serves as a step-by-step guide, providing a roadmap for individuals seeking to forge a new path and find fulfillment in their professional lives.

First Responders Who Found Fulfillment in Alternative Paths

In the fast-paced and demanding fields of athletics and first response, many professionals find themselves contemplating a career transition at some point in their lives. Whether it's due to a desire for a change of pace, the need for a new challenge, or simply a shift in personal priorities, the journey to discovering a new path can be both exciting and daunting.

For athletes, transitioning from a life dedicated to sports can be particularly challenging. The structured routines, high-pressure environments, and intense physical demands that come with being a professional athlete can make it difficult to envision a life beyond the game. However, countless athletes have found fulfillment and success in alternative paths, leveraging their unique skill sets and competitive mindset to excel in new endeavors.

Similarly, first responders often face unique challenges when contemplating a career change. The demanding nature of their work, coupled with the emotional toll it can take, can make it difficult to imagine a life outside of the world of emergency services. Yet, many first responders have discovered new passions and purposes in alternative career paths, channeling their natural problem-solving abilities and dedication to service into new endeavors.

Their journeys serve as a guide for mid-career professionals, lawyers, doctors, and anyone considering a change in career paths. Through their experiences, readers will gain valuable insights into the process of reinvention, including how to identify transferable skills, explore new industries, and build a network of support.

Additionally, this provides practical advice and actionable steps for those seeking to make a career transition. From developing a personal brand and crafting a compelling resume to honing interview skills and leveraging professional networks, readers will gain the tools they need to successfully navigate the job market and find fulfillment in alternative paths.

Ultimately, "First Responders Who Found Fulfillment in Alternative Paths" offers a roadmap for athletes, first responders, and professionals alike who are seeking to make a change. By learning from the experiences of those who have successfully transitioned, readers can gain the confidence and inspiration needed to embark on their own journey of reinvention.

Mid-career professionals, Lawyers, and Doctors Who Made Successful Transitions

In today's rapidly changing world, career transitions have become a common occurrence. Many individuals find themselves seeking new paths and exploring different professional opportunities. This subchapter is dedicated to mid-career professionals, lawyers, and doctors who have successfully made transitions in their careers, providing inspiration and guidance for athletes, first responders, and others looking to change their career paths.

Transitioning from one career to another can be a daunting task, especially for individuals who have invested significant time and effort in their current professions. However, the stories of those who have successfully navigated these transitions can serve as a source of motivation and guidance for those seeking change.

One such example is Dr. Sarah Johnson, a renowned surgeon who remarkably transitioned from the medical field to entrepreneurship. Driven by her passion for innovation and creating solutions, she founded a medical technology start-up that revolutionized the industry. Her story serves as a testament to the fact that it is never too late to pursue a new career and make a significant impact.

Similarly, John Anderson, a successful lawyer, found himself yearning for a more fulfilling career that aligned with his personal values. He made the courageous decision to transition into the nonprofit sector, where he now advocates for social justice and equality. His journey showcases that finding purpose and fulfillment in a new career is possible, even after establishing oneself in a different field.

For mid-career professionals seeking to make a transition, it is essential to recognize that transferable skills and experiences can be leveraged to ease the process.

Lawyers, for instance, possess excellent analytical, research, and communication skills that can be applied to various industries. By identifying these transferable skills and exploring new areas of interest, lawyers can successfully transition into fields such as consulting, entrepreneurship, or even politics.

Doctors, on the other hand, can utilize their medical knowledge and expertise to pursue careers in medical writing, healthcare consulting, or medical education. The ability to combine their medical background with other interests can lead to exciting and fulfilling career opportunities.

This highlights the stories of mid-career professionals, lawyers, and doctors who have made successful transitions in their careers. Their journeys serve as a source of inspiration for athletes, first responders, and others looking to change career paths. By leveraging transferable skills and exploring new areas of interest, individuals can pave the way for a fulfilling and prosperous second career. Remember, it is never too late to chase your dreams and embark on a new professional journey.

Chapter 14 – Creating a Sustainable and Fulfilling Career Path

Aligning Your Career with Your Personal Values and Passions

In order to lead a fulfilling and successful life, it is crucial to align your career with your personal values and passions. This subchapter will guide athletes, first responders, mid-career professionals, lawyers, and doctors through the process of changing career paths and finding a vocation that resonates with their true selves.

Discovering Your Personal Values -

The first step towards aligning your career with your personal values and passions is to identify what truly matters to you. Take the time to reflect on your core beliefs, principles, and the things that bring you joy and fulfillment. For athletes and first responders, transitioning to a new career can be daunting, but understanding your values will help you navigate this journey with clarity and purpose.

Assessing Your Passions and Interests -

Identifying your passions and interests is essential when exploring new career paths. Consider the activities, hobbies, or causes that ignite a fire within you. Whether it is helping others, pursuing creative endeavors, or making a positive impact on society, recognizing your passions will guide you towards a fulfilling career.

Researching Potential Career Paths -

Once you have a clear understanding of your values and passions, it is time to explore potential career paths that align with them. Conduct thorough research on industries, job roles, and organizations that resonate with your interests. Seek out mentors, attend networking events, and engage in informational interviews to gain insights into different fields and determine which ones align most closely with your values and passions.

Building the Necessary Skills -

Changing career paths often requires acquiring new skills or enhancing existing ones. Identify the skills needed for your desired career and invest in professional development opportunities. This may involve enrolling in courses, pursuing advanced degrees, or seeking mentorship from industry professionals. Building a solid skill set will increase your confidence and open doors to new opportunities.

Taking Calculated Risks -

Transitioning to a new career path may involve taking calculated risks. It is important to acknowledge and overcome any fears or doubts you may have. Seek support from mentors, family, and friends who can provide guidance and encouragement throughout your journey. Embrace the uncertainty and trust the process, knowing that aligning your career with your personal values and passions will ultimately lead to a more fulfilling and purposeful life.

Aligning your career with your personal values and passions is a transformative process that empowers athletes, first responders, mid-career professionals, lawyers, and doctors to find true fulfillment in their work. By recognizing and embracing your values, exploring passions, researching potential career paths, building necessary skills, and taking calculated risks, you can embark on a new journey that aligns with your authentic self. Remember, it is never too late to change career paths and create a life that brings you joy, satisfaction, and a sense of purpose.

Embracing Lifelong Learning and Adaptability

In today's fast-paced and ever-changing world, the ability to adapt and learn throughout our lives has become a crucial skill. Whether you are an athlete, a first responder, a mid-career professional, a lawyer, or a doctor, embracing lifelong learning and adaptability is essential for successful career transitions and personal growth. This subchapter will explore the importance of these qualities and provide practical strategies for embracing them.

One of the critical reasons why lifelong learning is vital is the rapid evolution of industries and technologies. What may have been a successful career path a decade ago may no longer be viable today.

As an athlete, you have already experienced the need for adaptation, constantly honing your skills and staying up-to-date with the latest training techniques. The same principle applies to professionals in other fields as well. By embracing lifelong learning, you will not only remain relevant but also open doors to new opportunities and career paths.

Adaptability goes hand in hand with lifelong learning. Being able to adapt to new situations, challenges, and environments is a valuable skill that can make career transitions smoother. As a first responder, you have likely encountered numerous unpredictable situations that require quick thinking and adaptability. Similarly, lawyers and doctors face ever-changing laws and medical advancements that necessitate continuous learning and adaptability to provide the best possible services to their clients and patients.

To embrace lifelong learning and adaptability, it is essential to cultivate a growth mindset. This mindset involves believing in your ability to learn and improve throughout your life, regardless of your current skills or knowledge. It requires being open to new ideas, seeking out opportunities for growth, and being willing to step out of your comfort zone.

Practical strategies for embracing lifelong learning and adaptability include staying curious, seeking out new experiences, and investing in personal development. This can involve attending workshops, conferences, and seminars, enrolling in online courses, joining professional networks, or even pursuing higher education or certifications. Additionally, cultivating a robust support system and surrounding yourself with like-minded individuals who value continuous learning can be immensely beneficial.

Embracing lifelong learning and adaptability is crucial for athletes, first responders, mid-career professionals, lawyers, and doctors. By continuously learning and adapting, you will not only thrive in your current career but also be prepared for any career transitions that may come your way. Embrace the mindset of lifelong learning, seek out new experiences, and invest in personal development to ensure a successful and fulfilling professional journey.

Finding Fulfillment and Satisfaction in Your Chosen Path

In today's fast-paced and ever-changing world, it is not uncommon for individuals to find themselves questioning their chosen career paths.

Whether you are an athlete looking to transition into a new career, a first responder seeking a change, a mid-career professional feeling stuck, or a lawyer or doctor considering a shift, the journey to finding fulfillment and satisfaction in your chosen path can be daunting.

The first step towards changing career paths is self-reflection. Take the time to evaluate your interests, passions, and values. What truly makes you happy? What gets you excited to wake up every morning? Identifying these aspects will help guide you toward a career that aligns with your authentic self.

Once you have a clear understanding of what you want, it is essential to conduct thorough research. Explore different industries, job roles, and opportunities that match your interests. Contact professionals in those fields and ask for informational interviews or shadowing experiences. This will provide you with invaluable insights and help you determine if a particular career path is the right fit for you.

Transitioning to a new career often requires acquiring additional skills or education. Embrace the opportunity to learn and grow. Take advantage of online courses, workshops, or certifications to enhance your knowledge and qualifications in your desired field.

Additionally, consider networking events and industry conferences to connect with like-minded professionals who can offer guidance and support during your career transition.

Embracing a growth mindset is crucial when changing career paths. It is natural to face obstacles and setbacks along the way, but these should be viewed as opportunities for growth rather than roadblocks. Maintain a positive attitude and remain resilient in the face of challenges. Surround yourself with a supportive network of family, friends, and mentors who can provide encouragement and guidance throughout your journey.

Remember that finding fulfillment and satisfaction in your chosen path is a continuous process. As you evolve and grow, your interests and goals may change. Embrace the journey and remain open to new possibilities. Regularly reassess your career path and make adjustments as needed to ensure you are consistently aligned with your true calling.

Finding fulfillment and satisfaction in your chosen path requires self-reflection, research, continuous learning, a growth mindset, and a supportive network. Whether you are an athlete, first responder, mid-career professional, lawyer, or doctor, embracing the process of changing career paths can lead to a more fulfilling and satisfying professional life.

Conclusion – Your Playbook for Athlete Career Transitions

Congratulations! You have reached the conclusion of our step-by-step guide, "The Playbook for Athlete Career Transitions." Throughout this journey, we have explored the unique challenges and opportunities that athletes face when transitioning from their sports careers to new professional paths. Whether you are an athlete, a first responder, a mid-career professional, a lawyer, or a doctor, this playbook has provided you with the tools and strategies to navigate this exciting yet daunting transition successfully.

Changing career paths can be a daunting task, especially for individuals who have dedicated their lives to sports or other demanding professions. However, armed with the knowledge and insights from this playbook, you are now equipped to tackle this new chapter in your life confidently.

One of the key takeaways from this guide is the importance of self-reflection and self-assessment. Understanding your skills, values, and passions will help you identify potential career paths that align with your interests and strengths.

By engaging in this reflective process, you will be able to create a solid foundation for your transition and set yourself up for success.

Another critical aspect of career transition is developing a solid professional network. Throughout this playbook, we have emphasized the significance of networking and building relationships within your desired industry. Connecting with individuals who have successfully transitioned from a similar background can provide invaluable guidance and support. Don't be afraid to reach out and seek mentorship or advice – you'll be surprised at how willing people are to help.

We have explored the importance of acquiring new skills and education. While your previous experiences may be valuable, it is essential to continuously learn and adapt to the demands of your new career. Embracing opportunities for growth and development, whether through online courses, workshops, or formal education, will enhance your marketability and open doors to new possibilities.

We cannot stress enough the significance of perseverance and resilience. Transitioning careers can be challenging, and setbacks are inevitable. However, by maintaining a positive mindset, staying focused on your goals, and persisting through obstacles, you will overcome any hurdles that come your way.

This playbook is not an endpoint but a starting point for your career transition. Embrace the process, be open to new opportunities, and continue to learn and grow. You have the power to create a fulfilling career beyond your athletic or current profession. Good luck on your journey, may it be filled with new adventures and endless possibilities!

www.ingramcontent.com/pod-product-compliance
Lightning Source LLC
Chambersburg PA
CBHW071054290526

45795CB00004B/1484